MORE PEOPLE!

IS CHURCH GROWTH WORTH IT?

Nelson Annan

Harold Shaw Publishers
Wheaton, Illinois

ISBN 0–87788–552–4

Library of Congress Cataloging-in-Publication Data
Annan, Nelson.
More people!

1. Church growth. I. Title.
BV652.25.A54 1987 254'.5 87-20526
ISBN 0-87788-552-4

96 95 94 93 92 91 90 89 88 87

10 9 8 7 6 5 4 3 2 1

More People!
Is Church Growth Worth It?

CONTENTS

Preface

Two American sportsmen on a moose hunting expedition were flown into the northern wilderness by sea plane. Their Canadian bush pilot skillfully landed on a small lake and deposited the hunters on shore with their gear.

Just before leaving, the pilot warned them: "This lake is small, and the trees on the shore are very tall. It's difficult to take off with a full load. Remember that no matter how many moose you see this week, we can take only one moose with us on the plane."

A week later the pilot returned for the hunters, who, much to the pilot's dismay, had killed two moose.

The pilot exploded, "I told you only one moose!"

But one of the hunters replied, "Last year our pilot let us take out two moose."

The bush pilot bristled. He prided himself on being the best in the business. "Same kind of plane?" he asked.

"Yep."

"Same lake?"

"Yep."

"He was a fool," the pilot said at last. "But if he could do it, so can I."

The hunters packed all their gear and the two moose into the soon overloaded seaplane. Cranking the engine to its limit, the pilot took off. But the bulging plane hit the top of several fir trees on the far shore. Plane, moose meat, and hunters were scattered across the forest.

One of the hunters shook himself, slowly stood up, and in a shaky voice, asked his buddy, "Hey, Hank! Where are we?"

"I don't know," he replied. "But I think we're about 100 feet farther than we made it last year."

Like those foolish hunters, we're often determined to do it our way, no matter how many times we fail. We have a tendency to follow the seven last words of the church: "But we've always done it this way!"

During the last three years as I have lectured and published articles about church growth, I have been encouraged by hundreds of Christians who responded positively by saying, "Yes, we *do* want to fulfill Christ's Great Commission for this community. We want to improve. We are tired of doing things the same way with the same lack of results."

But if the condition of the church is to improve, local leaders and individual Christians must recognize the stunted growth in many congregations.

I believe our Lord Jesus is saying to many of our churches, "I know your deeds; you have a reputation of being alive, but you are dead. Wake up! Strengthen what remains and is about to die, for I have not found your deeds complete in the sight of my God. Remember, therefore, what you have received, and heard; obey it, and repent" (Rev. 3:1-3).

This book is for anyone who wants to respond to our Lord's challenge. Since the principles apply to almost any church, I hope it will benefit Christians across a wide spectrum. I pray that individual believers and leaders who are interested in making a difference in their own churches will take the time to read, study, and discuss the concepts presented in this book.

Nelson Annan

Acknowledgments

I am grateful to James Stahr who first believed that my church growth lectures were worth publishing in *Interest* magazine; to Bruce McNicol and Bill Conard who pursued publication of this book; to Joanne Bell for typing and editing the initial manuscript; to Susan Holton, and David and Reneé Sanford for thoroughly polishing the text; to Harold Westing who has taught me much about church growth; and to my dear wife, Jan, my co-worker and best friend.

Study Suggestions

To get the most from this book you may wish to read, study, and discuss it with other leaders and members in your local church.

At the end of each chapter you will find study questions to help you review and apply key concepts. Church leaders particularly may wish to use these questions to guide their study discussions.

You may wish to plan your study around the book's three major sections. Allow one or two sessions to discuss section one and approximately twice as much time to discuss sections two and three.

I

Expectations for Growth

1

New Testament Churches Grow!

DID YOU KNOW that today God is bringing more people to faith in Jesus Christ than at any other time in history? Around the world, the church is growing at a phenomenal pace! Rejoice as you consider that:

- Every day in China an estimated 27,000 people become Christians.
- The Protestant church in The Philippines is doubling in size every seven to eight years.
- Evangelicals soon will comprise fifty percent of Guatemala's population.

God's church, inspired by God's Spirit, is on the move! Christians are planning for church growth as never before. What an exciting time to serve Christ the King! The church is on the move, yet the task is barely begun.

Today many claim that North America, particularly the United States, is experiencing a great resurgence of "born again" faith. But of the 250 million people in the U.S., 100 million have no active religious affiliation, and at least 75 million others are Christians in name only. Thus more than 175 million in the U.S.—including many people you know—have not yet received Christ. You may be surprised to discover that there are more non-Christians in this country than in most other nations. What a challenge Christians face today!

Yet in the face of such need, many churches are still not growing. Number-wise, we simply do not have enough churches to reach our country with the gospel. In 1900 the U.S. had twenty-seven churches for every 10,000 people. Today we have only twelve churches for every 10,000 people. An estimated eighty to eighty-five percent of all North American churches are either static in growth or are declining.

As Christians we should be excited by what God is doing and challenged by the millions around us who need Christ. But what are our churches doing to reach these millions? I conducted an informal survey of seventeen Brethren assemblies and found that fourteen were seeing fewer than two adult conversions annually. Another survey of twenty-three congregations found the same lack of growth. A survey of churches in England reported that forty percent had seen no conversions in the previous two years!

The evidence is overwhelming. Most of us are sadly aware that most churches aren't growing. Yet, if we are to model our churches after New Testament principles, we *must* grow. The New Testament speaks directly to this matter.

The Lord Jesus' final challenge to his disciples—words meant to ring in their ears—is a call for church growth. Significantly, this Great Commission is included in each of the four Gospels and in Acts (Matthew 28:18-20; Mark 16:15; Luke 24:46-49; John 20:21; Acts 1:8). Christ's mandate comes through loud and clear: The church of Jesus Christ is expected to march on and *multiply,* not simply to maintain.

It's no accident that in the Book of Acts Luke focuses our attention on the growth of the early church. From the day of Pentecost, the church multiplied at an incredible rate. When reading Acts 2 in the past, I used to focus solely on verse 42, which emphasizes four marks of the New Testament church: the apostles' doctrine, fellowship, breaking of bread, and prayer. But in this passage Luke also mentions numerous conversions and baptisms, generosity and sharing, and gladness and praise (Acts 2:41, 43-47). And in this context Luke emphasizes numerical growth *twice.*

The Holy Spirit inspired Luke to write about church growth. "Those who accepted his message were baptized, and about three thousand were *added to their number* that day" (v. 41), and the Christians were "praising God and enjoying the favor of all the people. And *the Lord added to their number daily* those who were being saved" (v. 47).

Clearly God *is* interested in numbers. God *is* interested in growth. How then can you claim to be a New Testament church if you are not growing? The growth that Luke records in Acts was a vital part of early church life:

> "But many who heard the message believed, and the number of men grew to about five thousand" (Acts 4:4).

> "Nevertheless, more and more men and women believed in the Lord and were added to their number" (Acts 5:14).

"So the word of God spread. The number of disciples in Jerusalem increased rapidly, and a large number of priests became obedient to the faith" (Acts 6:7).

"Then the church throughout Judea, Galilee and Samaria enjoyed a time of peace. It was strengthened; and encouraged by the Holy Spirit, it grew in numbers, living in the fear of the Lord" (Acts 9:31).

"The Lord's hand was with them, and a great number of people believed and turned to the Lord" (Acts 11:21).

"So the churches were strengthened in the faith and grew daily in numbers" (Acts 16:5).

Clearly the New Testament church described by Luke in the Book of Acts was a growing church. Is your church growing? I hope so. Whether your church is growing or not, I pray this book will challenge, encourage and move you toward new growth or even greater growth in your own congregation.

Study Questions

1. "Around the world, the church is growing at a phenomenal pace." At what pace has your church grown in the last ten years? How fast is it growing today? How fast might it grow during the next decade?

2. "There are more non-Christians in this country than in most other nations." What is the greatest challenge facing North American churches today? In what ways is your congregation currently responding to that challenge?

3. "If we are to be true New Testament churches, we must grow." How would you define a growing church? How much would you like to see your fellowship grow during the next twelve months?

4. "From the day of Pentecost, the church multiplied at an incredible rate." What prompted such rapid growth? For how long did this rapid growth pattern continue? What prompts significant church growth today? What factors do you think might hinder a congregation from growing?

2

Why Isn't My Church Growing?

FIRST-CENTURY CHRISTIANS were deeply concerned about church growth. Under the Holy Spirit's direction, they constantly searched for new ways to build churches and to help them spread the gospel around the world. But over the centuries Christians haven't kept up with that growth rate. Why?

Churches don't grow for four basic reasons. Two factors may be beyond their control, but virtually all churches wrestle with one or two problems they *can* do something about. Let's examine these four reasons for this widespread lack of church growth.

Unresponsive Fields

A church located in an unresponsive field—such as a Jewish or Muslim neighborhood—may not grow rapidly no matter how strong its outreach programs are. Reaching certain people groups is very difficult. Thus, a dynamic church in such a community may experience very slow growth.

Today's small, rural towns make up another unresponsive field. In many such communities, the population declines as youth and families move to the cities. A church located in one of these towns may have a valid reason for not growing rapidly: You can't reach people who aren't there!

High Mobility Communities

Churches located in high mobility communities may be leading people to Christ, bringing them into the congregation, and then seeing these new people soon move on to another community. This occurs most often in areas surrounding a university, military base, or certain major industries. Although a local fellowship may be reaching out and discipling young men and women and families, the congregation may find it difficult to sustain its numerical growth due to high mobility.

Carnality and Sin

However, the majority of North American churches are not located in unresponsive or high mobility communities. For some congregations, the problems affecting growth lie within the body of believers.

Scripture teaches that God may take his hand from a church if its members indulge in carnality and sin, if its people are divided, or if its people have cold hearts. Christ gives this warning to five of the seven churches addressed in Revelation 2 and 3: Unless a congregation repents and obeys God, he will take away his blessing. If sin dominates the leadership or life of a church, why should God bring further numerical growth?

Every church should heed God's warning to the church in Laodicea (Rev. 3:14-22). The Christians in the Laodicean church were comfortable and orthodox, but God condemned them as being "wretched, pitiful, poor, blind, and naked" (v. 17). Through sin a church can grow cold without realizing it.

Wrong Methods and Wrong Thinking

More than three-fourths of all North American churches are not growing. The problem is epidemic! In many cases the failure to grow is not a result of carnality and sin, but of wrong methods and wrong thinking.

For instance, many churches become content with a *sowing* mentality when they should strive for a *reaping* mentality. In response to the Great Commission, we distribute tracts, organize Vacation Bible Schools, and present the gospel every Sunday. Although we are mildly disturbed when so few trust Christ through our efforts, we are satisfied (because of our sowing mentality) that at least we have been faithful.

In contrast, growing churches develop a reaping mentality. They see God saving people around the world. They believe that God wants to save people *now,* where they live, with their help. They take time to examine perspectives and methods. They long for change. They refuse to be satisfied with simply sharing the gospel. They *expect* God to bring a great harvest through their local church. And they are willing to work diligently to help it happen, just like the Christians in the first century.

Study Questions

1. "Churches don't grow for four basic reasons." To what degree do each of these factors currently limit your own church's rate of growth? Which factor most affects your congregation?

2. "For many congregations, the problems affecting growth lie within the body of believers." How are such problems identified and corrected within your congregation?

3. "Growing churches . . . expect God to bring a great harvest through their local church." How much harvest do church leaders expect to see in your congregation this year? What have you and others been doing during the last year to reap a harvest? How effective has each effort been?

3

Big vs. Small: Some Misconceptions

MOST NORTH AMERICAN CHURCHES should be growing, but aren't. Why not? Their growth may be stunted by carnality or some hidden internal sin. But first we need to consider the mindset or mentality that dictates their activities. For many groups, one or more misconceptions are stunting their numerical and spiritual growth. As you read these seven false assumptions, ask yourself this question: Have any of them ever been a part of your thinking about your church?

Misconception #1

In order to grow, a church must become more spiritual.

Some churches have an inferiority complex. They assume that another congregation grows because its people are more spiritual. So when someone asks, "How can we be a growing church?" their response focuses on spiritual qualifications: "We need to study the Word more" or "We should pray more" or "If we were holier people, God would bless us and we would grow."

All of these statements hold some truth. Chapters 2 and 3 of Revelation warn us that churches lose vitality because of spiritual decline. Scripture calls us to holiness, prayer, and the Word. God wants us to be more like his Son and fashioned into his image.

But some congregations have been seeking to become more spiritual for twenty years—and still they aren't growing! Whether they just talk about it or actually do pray and study more, these local churches are not growing. The need for deeper spiritual life becomes an excuse for not reaching their community for Christ.

We don't need to attain a certain measure of perfection before God can use us. Church growth usually isn't a matter of super-spirituality or superior commitment to Christ. To discover this, visit several growing churches in your community. I suspect that you will not find deeper spiritual life, but rather a strong commitment to grow.

Misconception #2
Growing churches are less spiritual.
Some churches that don't wrestle with the first misconception struggle with this opposite but equally false assumption. Comparing themselves with other local churches who are experiencing growth, some critics in static churches say, "They don't pay attention to biblical principles like we do. If we lowered our standards, then we would grow" or, "If we weren't as pure and faithful to the Word, we'd grow too!"

Like the first misconception, this one has some elements of truth. Anyone can gather a good crowd with the right kind of show. Someone once said, "Getting a crowd is not an accomplishment; it's an opportunity." With a little effort you could double the numbers at your church within a few weeks! You could bring in three major league professional athletes this week. The following week you might offer a $20 bill to every visitor. The third week you could promise that if fifty visitors come, your elder will stand on the platform and swallow a live goldfish. Then you could sit back and watch the numbers increase!

But is that the way God calls us to pursue growth? Some churches use well-intentioned but misguided tricks to draw big crowds. But most growing churches don't resort to such gimmicks. You are making a false assumption when you attribute your congregation's lack of growth to your spiritual superiority. God calls us to humbly admit our pride and our mistakes and then challenges us to move on from there.

If God loves the world—and he does—and if God commands evangelism—and he does—then failing to win souls to Christ may put us at the bottom of the spiritual ladder. We must admit and confess our disobedience to him, and then take action to change our focus.

If a church maintains this false sense of superiority, thinking it doesn't grow because it refuses to drop its standards, I believe God will confront its members, saying: "I love these people who are dying, but you fail to love them. I commanded you to evangelize, but you fail to evangelize. Instead of seeing yourselves as spiritually superior, confess your failure and need, and I will give you strength to do what you cannot do on your own."

Today many kinds of churches—including many conservative, biblical churches—are growing. It *can* take place. Failure to grow is not a sign of spiritual superiority. Don't allow this mistaken perspective to keep your church from growing.

Misconception #3
Emphasizing quantity dilutes a commitment to quality.

Small congregations may justify their size by saying, "You can't have both quality and quantity. We are committed to quality. We may be small, but we have biblical teaching, biblical worship, and biblical fellowship. That's what really counts."

True, sometimes quality is sacrificed when we grow numerically. A growth-oriented church may be so program-oriented that it becomes superficial.

But quantity and quality don't have to be mutually exclusive. God doesn't want us to choose between the two; he wants us to strive for both. Because growth is both spiritual and numerical, our churches must grow in both quality *and* quantity.

Quality churches can and will grow. Ask God to help you: "Lord, we want to *grow up* into maturity. We want to become the kind of fellowship described in Ephesians 4:14-16. Lord, we want to *grow together.* We want to be a unified church. Lord, we want to *grow out* in evangelism. We want to grow up, grow together, and grow out as we reach the world for Jesus Christ."

With God's help, churches can achieve all three at the same time!

Misconception #4
People who leave one congregation to join another lack spirituality and commitment to biblical principles.

This mistaken perspective about church growth—or the lack of it—focuses attention on those who "defect" from our ranks. It assumes that those who leave are to blame, not those who remain. Yet church growth depends not only on winning new people, but also on keeping the ones you have!

Some humorously call this fourth misconception "remnant theology." Perhaps you feel like the remnant left in Judah after the Babylonians took all the important Jews in three separate hostage incidents. Only you, the holy remnant, remain. You might say of the defectors: "Joe joined this other church, and Sue and her husband are going to that one across town. It's a shame they weren't as committed to biblical principles as we are."

This explanation for lack of church growth has some truth to it. Read 2 Timothy 4:10. Demas is an example. Or read 1 John 2:19 about the people who left because "they did not really belong to us." This is true of certain defectors—some people may feel out of place at your church. Church growth studies consistently show that non-growing churches don't lose people because the defectors are less spiritual, but because these static churches are filled with hidden signs which read: "Not welcome."

Every church—even yours—has these signs. Look for them. Not having a wheelchair ramp is a sign that reads: "Handicapped people are not welcome here." That particular problem is harder to solve in older buildings, but new facilities should be designed to accommodate wheelchairs.

The sign "Young parents are not welcome" is created by dingy or non-existent nursery facilities. Any mother with young children will see that sign—in neon lights—and probably not return. If the Christian education program of a church is outdated, parents will take their families where the program meets today's need with a more contemporary application.

When our congregation was experiencing some growth pains and we began talking about enlarging our building, we took down some of our "not welcome" signs. I was delighted when a man in our congregation admitted, "I always believed that those who came for only a few months and then left did so because they weren't committed. Now I realize that we failed to welcome newcomers."

This important insight changed that man's entire attitude. Many of us need to learn the same lesson and stop passing the blame.

Recently, a leader in a dynamic, growing church in Colorado mentioned to me that a number of couples had recently left their fellowship. I suggested that he ask the couples *why* they went elsewhere. He determined that he would make some personal visits to find out.

When I visited that congregation later, the man told me he had met with a number of the families which no longer attended there. How much he had learned! The insightful conversations they shared helped him to recognize several weaknesses, which the church immediately corrected.

All congregations lose some people out the back door. But growing churches discover *why* people leave so they can correct the problems. Church growth studies call this "closing the back door." When people leave your church fellowship don't be afraid to ask for specifics: "*What* did we do wrong? *How* did we fail to love or serve you as we should?"

We can learn a great deal by speaking with those who have left. Often we'll realize that they didn't leave because they are less spiritual or less committed. Many times the problem is ours, not theirs. So let's listen with open minds and then do some honest searching about how we can practically "close the back door."

Misconception #5
Big churches are weaker, less friendly, and less spiritual.

These claims are partly true. A small congregation may be

more personal and more effective than a large one. A church of forty or fifty people shares an intimacy that larger groups cannot duplicate. However, your church may not be as personal as you think it is.

How many people in your congregation does the average member know by first name? Church growth studies indicate that the average person knows between forty and sixty people. If your church has 100 adults, you have more than most people can relate to on a first-name basis. The small personal feeling has already been diminished.

Many congregations fear size. And sadly, the myth that churches should divide when they reach a group of 200 has often led strong, growing fellowships to separate into weak and ineffective smaller groups.

A Brethren elder from another city told me a story I hear again and again. In their town they had one solid assembly. Because they began to grow, they divided and started a new fellowship. Now instead of one strong congregation they have two weak ones. Small churches are often weak, and suffer from a lack of strong leadership, preaching, teaching, and programming.

Misconception #6

It is faithfulness, not results, that counts.

1 Corinthians 4 teaches the importance of being faithful stewards. That's a basic New Testament truth. But the false assumption underlying this misconception is that because faithfulness is crucial, results are not important. We must realize that faithfulness is not the opposite of growth. When a church is truly faithful to the New Testament, *growth will follow.*

We have already discussed several church growth passages in Acts. Why did God give us that numerical emphasis? Because he cares about numbers.

Suppose a farmer has sown the same field for five years with little result. When asked about his harvest, he replies: "It's very poor. But I'm called only to sow. I leave the results to God." Most of us would encourage that farmer to re-examine his plowing methods, his fertilizer—anything! Something is definitely wrong with his sowing if he is not reaping anything at harvest time. The same principle applies in our churches. How can we do the same thing year after year with no results and shrug, "We leave the results to God"?

God holds us responsible as laborers in his harvest. If we intend to reap, we must first examine our attitudes and methods.

Misconception #7
There is one simple answer why a church is not growing.

Many people are attracted to simple answers. They say, "The problem is . . ." and fill in anything that's quick and easy to understand. But solving lack of growth in our congregations is not that simple. Church growth requires more than pat answers.

The "answer" to your church's problem isn't just that you need to preach the gospel more, or that you need a new building, or that you need to pray more. An analysis of any church is complex. The solution to lack of growth almost certainly involves several factors.

Growth is not easy, but it is possible. Changing the factors that hinder growth takes time and effort, but the results make it worthwhile. My prayer is that all of us will want to make the changes necessary to become growing fellowships—the kind of churches God wants us to be.

Study Questions

1. "For many groups . . . one or more misconceptions are stunting their numerical and spiritual growth." Which of the seven false assumptions have you heard before? Which have been part of your own thinking? Which misconception seems most prevalent among Christians you know?

2. "Church growth usually isn't a matter of super-spirituality or superior commitment to Christ." Which congregations in your area are growing faster than your own? How do you feel about their measure of growth?

3. "Non-growing churches . . . are filled with hidden signs which read: 'Not welcome.' " How many "Not welcome" signs can you identify in your church? Who might be able to help make you aware of more hidden signs? What specific steps might your congregation take to remove these signs?

4

Saying "Yes!" to Church Growth

WHEN WE LIVED IN EDMONTON, Alberta, Canada's most northerly major city, our three children walked to and from school—even during the winter when temperatures often dipped below zero. One extremely cold day, my wife and I instructed Jeannie and Steven, then ages eight and five, to ride home from school on the city bus with their older brother, Kent.

After school Jeannie and Steven couldn't find Kent, so they boarded the city bus alone. Their ride should have taken five minutes. As dusk fell and temperatures dropped, we prayed and waited anxiously. I drove the route between our home and the school to look for them. My wife, Jan, called every home where they might have stopped on the way, but no one had seen the children.

As the night grew darker, I phoned the police. Just as I was describing Jeannie and Steven over the phone, they walked into our back yard! They had boarded the wrong bus and hadn't known where to get off. Uncertain of their destination, they remained on the bus until they had gone the entire route. With the driver's help they went around again until they found a familiar landmark, and walked the short distance home in the blowing snow.

Obviously, we all found the incident upsetting, especially Jeannie. She had been frightened when she was lost. But what really bothered her was that her little brother, tired after a long day at school and wrapped in a heavy snowsuit, had fallen asleep on the bus. She had felt all alone, unsure how to get home.

Some of you may feel like that in your congregation. Your destination—the kind of church you should become—is not very clear. And many people in your church seem to be sleeping, unconcerned that you are not growing. Either they are unaware of the problem, or they have lost hope that you can grow.

If your church is to grow, its people must capture a vision for growth. They must wake up and discover where they are headed. Growing churches not only *desire* growth, they *expect* it. They plan for growth. They have a vision for growth—and the faith that God will use them and will work in their midst.

Ask yourself: "How badly do we want to grow?" Obvious question, you say? Not really. Although all of us are committed to evangelism, at least in theory, many of us, in our hearts, really don't want to grow. It's easy to say, "We have enough people right now. I like our group of 100" or, "I feel more comfortable in a small group of fifty."

If we are content with our small size, is it so surprising that many churches aren't growing? If we enjoy being small, we probably will not grow. We won't work hard to gain what we don't want—*more people.*

Do you want your church to grow? Truly? Do you care about the world's lost people the way God cares about them? Are you content in a comfortable, but non-growing congregation even though God loves the world and has commanded you to win others to Christ? Be honest with yourself.

If you aren't growing, it may be difficult to capture a vision for church growth. I challenge you to pray: "God, give me the faith to believe you can cause our church to grow. Work in us to reach our world for Christ. Give us a vision for growth. Help us share that vision. Give our leaders a holy dissatisfaction with our complacency and a deep desire for growth."

Many of us have been lost or sleeping far too long. It's time Christians everywhere say "Yes!" to church growth.

Study Questions

1. "If your church is to grow, its people must capture a vision for growth." How many individuals in your congregation want and expect growth? How many people still lack a vision for growth?

2. "We must ask ourselves: 'How badly do we want to grow?' " Why do you want your congregation to grow? Why might some people be reluctant to see it grow?

3. "It's time Christians everywhere say 'Yes!' to church growth." Do you agree? Why or why not?

4. What do you hope to learn as you read, study, and discuss the rest of this book?

II

Directions for Growth

5

20/20 Vision for Church Growth

DEVELOPING A CLEAR VISION for growth is absolutely essential if your church wants to be a growing one. If we don't look at our individual churches with 20/20 perception first, all our best-laid plans for growth may become blurred and unusable.

But before we can examine essential factors for growth, we need to define the term "church growth." We are very familiar with the terminology, but what exactly does it mean? Let's look at two definitions:

1. "Church growth" is effective evangelism resulting in the numerical increase of born-again believers who are active in the local church.

2. "Church growth" is all that is involved in bringing people to know Christ, and then bringing them into responsible church fellowship.

Some people react negatively when church growth is mentioned. They immediately think of less-than-biblical evangelism or gimmicks to create a crowd, as we discussed in chapter three. But take another look at the two definitions above. Surely those who love God and study the Bible should agree that this kind of church growth pleases God.

If you believe that New Testament churches should grow and that God wants to bring that growth through you, you need to identify the directions essential for church growth. What can you do to involve your congregation in the bigger picture—the church growth happening around the world?

Look through a Visitor's Eyes

As two church members visited homes to invite people to their church, they met an epileptic man who said he would like to attend but feared his epilepsy might cause problems. The members assured him that he would be given a special chair, and that if he had a seizure, the ushers would carry him out in the chair, avoiding embarrassment.

The following Sunday the ushers led the visitor to his special seat. When the congregation stood to sing, the man's chair was accidentally pushed back, and when everyone sat down, he fell sprawling to the floor. Believing the man was having a seizure, the ushers ran to him, stuffed a large handkerchief into his mouth, and with great efficiency carried him into the foyer. When they let go of him, the man jumped up and raced out the door, leaving his coat behind.

The incident was unfortunate, but this church didn't quit

easily. The aggressive visitation pair visited him that afternoon to return his coat. To their amazement their epileptic friend hadn't visited their church at all that morning. And the other man? He never returned to get his coat!

Funny story, you say? How many churches have unwittingly made visitors feel almost as uncomfortable as the poor "epileptic" above? Do visitors feel welcome and relaxed in your church? Is parking a hassle? Is the sign out front legible and freshly painted? Or does the sign's peeling paint tell visitors: "We don't expect anyone to be attracted to us, so we don't try to attract anyone."

Does someone stand at the door to welcome visitors with a smile? Does an usher help visitors find a seat? Are sensitive Christians directing parents with small children to the nursery or the right Sunday school class? Is the nursery clean and comfortable? No matter how small the congregation, visitors need friendly guidance.

Does the sloppy bulletin announce, "We are not excited about what happens here. We just slap this bulletin together because we've always done it this way"?

Does the preacher make people feel relaxed? Is he friendly? Do people feel that he is prepared and that the service is well planned? Do they sense a clear purpose in the service?

What are a visitor's first impressions? His mind may be made up before he hears the sermon. Studies indicate that most visitors decide within fifteen minutes after entering the building whether or not they will return. How does your church encourage visitors to return?

Like the familiar chips and cracks at home, we often tend to overlook the deficiencies of our building and services. But visitors don't. If you've attended your fellowship for several years, it may be difficult for you to evaluate your congregation objectively. Ask the newest person among you to help you take off the blinders of familiarity to see your church with a visitor's eyes.

Although people shouldn't "judge a book by its cover," publishers always give careful consideration to book covers. Why? Because people *do* judge a book by its cover—at least until they read it. Visitors naturally judge your church by their first impressions. If your "cover" is unappealing, why should they return?

Notice Areas of Strength

A church that wants to grow must not only *gain the vision* to grow, but must also *take action* to grow. Develop a game plan to bring growth. But before you can take action, you must evaluate further.

Look at your congregation's strengths. What do you do best? Almost all churches have some strong points. Identify these strengths through evaluation and then emphasize them.

If your youth group is a strong point, your church should invest its best people into youth work, promote it, and encourage those already involved in it. Inform newcomers and potential visitors about your great youth group. Advertise it. Your preaching may not be great, and your music may be nothing special. But don't emphasize the negative; *emphasize the positive.*

Do you have a fantastic women's Bible study group? Then talk about that. Announce it. Celebrate it! Encourage those involved in it.

Growing churches know and maximize their strengths. They can also turn their weaknesses into strengths. So don't apologize for your church. Don't say, "I wish we had a polished program like that large church over on Main Street, but we're just a tiny informal group." Instead present informality as a strength; it appeals to many people. Say, "If you want a church where the folks are friendly and you can be yourself, come visit us."

Seeing your church with 20/20 vision will help you not only to gain a vision for growth but to learn how to welcome visitors more effectively so that they'll come back again—and again! In the next chapter we'll study some ways to develop an atmosphere that encourages growth.

Study Questions

1. "Church growth is . . ." In your own words, how would you define church growth? How does your definition compare with the two definitions presented at the beginning of this chapter?

2. "Visitors judge your church by their first impressions." How does your "book cover" look? What improvements could be made within the next month?

3. "Growing churches maximize their strengths." What are your congregation's three strongest points? How might you communicate those strengths to visitors and others in your community?

6

Creating a Climate for Growth

DOES YOUR CHURCH have a growth climate? At prayer meetings do you pray, "God, help us reach people for Christ"? Do you talk about growth in your services? Do you recognize growth when it happens? Do you rejoice publicly when someone is born again? Is outreach a priority among your ministries? Do people sense from the church leadership that growth is expected, highly desired, and welcomed?

Questions and more questions! But you need to ask a lot of them. If visitors are to become regulars, you must create a growth climate which will make people want to join your group. How can this be accomplished?

Establish New Friendships

Is your congregation friendly to visitors or only to those who have been attending for years? Do you teach and encourage people to make others feel at home, or does everyone talk with their friends before and after the meetings so that no one has time to welcome visitors? How many people in your church reach out to visitors?

A recent Win Arn Growth Report (Number 13, 1986) reported that "the traditional American family is the exception, not the rule." Because there are not enough long-term families to meet people's needs, Americans have an increased need for friendships. The report concludes that churches which meet people's increased need for friendship "will find a receptivity of unequaled proportions."

The world needs loving churches where lonely people can find and experience God's love through God's people. This poem from *Who Cares About Love?* by Dr. Win Arn illustrates the importance of meeting each person's needs:

For want of love, a person was lost;
For want of a person, a family was lost;
For want of a family, a church was lost;
For want of a church, a community was lost;
For want of a community, a city was lost;
For want of a city, a state was lost;
For want of a state, a nation was lost;
For want of love . . .

No wonder friendship evangelism is emphasized today! People desperately need Jesus Christ, and they also need caring friends. Statistics indicate that seventy to eighty percent of those now attending church began attending through the influence of a friend or relative. Before people will attend your Sunday morning services, someone has to invite them.

Visitors should be impressed by your church's atmosphere of friendship, love, and acceptance. Jesus told the disciples, "A new command I give you: Love one another. As I have loved you, so you must love one another. All men will know that you are my disciples if you love one another" (John 13:34-35).

What do newcomers experience when they mingle with your congregation at a picnic, Christmas program, or Sunday morning service? Do they sense love among these Christians? Are they attracted to our Savior by this love? A perceptive man once said that we share the gospel not only through proclamation, but also through attraction. Our actions toward each other either draw people in or push them away.

A recent study indicates that good friendships weld new believers to the local church. The study found that new believers with five or more good friends in the local church continued attending, but those with very few or no Christian friends had a very high drop-out rate.

Nurture Body Life

Loving, friendly local churches are what Christ wants, what Christians need, and what attracts unbelievers to Christ. Churches must link the Great Commission (Matthew 28:18-20) and the Great Commandment (Mark 12:29-31). Christ wants us to "go and make disciples," to love God with all we've got, and to love our neighbors as ourselves.

Unfortunately, some of our churches are better in form than in real life. We say the right things, but we don't have the loving, supportive relationships of the early church. We may think we're friendly, while in fact, outsiders don't sense a loving atmosphere at all! If we desire to attract people to Christ, we must be sensitive to this problem and nurture body life. Here are six practical ways to nurture good relationships within your fellowship:

1. *Communicate love.* The leaders of the church should love people. But it doesn't always work out that way. Some church leaders may be strong in organizing, teaching, and leading committee meetings, but weak when it comes to relating to people.

   Leaders must not only love the flock, but communicate that love. All of us need to learn to communicate—with a smile, a compliment, a hand on the shoulder, or a hug—that we truly care about people. Loving churches have leaders who effectively communicate their love.

2. *Preach and teach love.* Suggest or select the subject of love for a series of sermons. Numerous Scripture passages speak of God's love for us and our love for each other. The person in the pulpit can challenge the church to grow in love for God, for one another, and for those around them. Consider showing one of the many excellent dramatic Christian films about love.

3. *Emphasize friendliness and warmth,* especially in greeting visitors. People-oriented greeters who smile, love to talk, and remember names should stand at the door to greet visitors. Use name tags at least periodically to help new people learn names. Ushers should be helpful and friendly.

4. *Follow up your visitors.* Does your congregation cultivate friendships with visitors? In loving churches that

have a growth perspective, a visitor may receive one or all of these follow-up gestures:

- a lunch invitation for that day or the next Sunday
- a telephone call that night saying, "We're glad you visited our church. Please return again soon."
- a letter received midweek to encourage them to return
- a visit on Thursday night by a couple who attempts to build the bridge of friendship and possibly share the gospel

If I visited your church next week, how many of these four gestures of friendship would I receive?

5. *Broaden the inner groups.* Loving churches make new people feel like they belong. When Christians who are new in the area begin to attend your meetings, are they assimilated quickly? Do people surround them in warmth and love? Do they have a group their own age in which to share their personal goals, interests, and needs? Do they feel welcome? That others' interest in them is genuine?

6. *Strengthen and increase social events.* We all need to spend time together in addition to Sunday services. If we seek to develop relationships, we need more than ten minutes before and after meetings. In loving churches, people spend time together outside of the church building.

Include everyone in your church's informal gatherings such as family nights, picnics, sports events, retreats, and holiday parties. Especially invite those who are new and may feel that these activities are for the regular attenders. Create unique ways to bring God's people together to play and laugh, to work and serve, and to learn and pray together.

Develop Small Groups

If more than forty adults attend your Sunday morning services, relationships can also be strengthened by small groups. People relate personally and openly to ten people in a way they cannot relate to fifty or more people. Friendships build and fellowship deepens when Christians gather in small groups.

Any small group can build loving relationships. Those involved in choir, Bible studies, church softball, or teaching Sunday school are enriched by the relationships they develop within their small groups.

Many churches have found that their mid-week prayer and Bible study groups have grown numerically and spiritually when they divided into home groups of ten or twenty people each. Group leaders should be taught to emphasize meaningful fellowship coupled with Bible study and prayer within these meetings so that the balance between social and spiritual doesn't become lopsided. Great relationships can grow out of these small groups—friendships that keep one-time visitors coming back.

Our aim should be to build church body life like that experienced by the New Testament Christians. When we build stronger loving relationships, God is glorified, Christians are strengthened, and unbelievers are attracted to God's love displayed in his people.

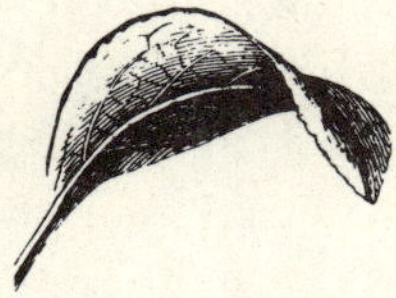

Study Questions

1. "Good friendships weld new believers to the local church." In what ways might your congregation better encourage members to establish friendships with visitors and new attendees?

2. "If you desire to attract people to Christ, you must nurture fellowship in the church." In what ways is your congregation already doing this? In what ways might your church relationships be enhanced?

3. "If more than forty adults attend your Sunday morning services, relationships can also be strengthened by small groups." Which small groups within your congregation already meet regularly? From what other types of small groups might your church benefit?

7

Igniting the Fires of Growth

THE BRILLIANT FIRE of church growth doesn't "happen" just by chance. Someone has to care enough to take the match, ignite the coals, and stand by patiently to tend the fire and keep it from dying down to cold ashes.

Growth takes time and concerned nurturing. Churches grow because they *plan* to grow, they *expect* to grow, and they *take steps* to grow. If your church desires to grow, your congregation must agree to work together to make it happen.

Let's discuss five guidelines to growth in your church:

Develop a Growth Program

Each church must develop a specific growth program. Every growing church has one, whether they recognize it or not.

Choose a program that produces results and works in your area and with your people. What is very effective in one community may be ineffective in yours. Find one that fits.

Our church effectively uses the Evangelism Explosion program which was begun by Dr. James Kennedy several decades ago and is now used by hundreds of churches around the world. It isn't perfect, but God has used this program mightily.

We began with two visitation teams of three people each who visited the homes of people who had visited our church. For the first several weeks no one professed faith in Christ through our efforts, but we persisted. Now between fifteen and twenty-five people visit homes every Tuesday night, and these visits sometimes result in two or three adults receiving Christ in a given week. Our visitation teams target the homes of Sunday visitors first, and then the homes of the children in our Bible club programs.

What fantastic results! In the past two years dozens of adults have professed faith in Jesus Christ when the gospel was presented by our teams. Those involved in the Evangelism Explosion program are well-equipped, and they expect Christ to change lives. And he does!

Churches know evangelism is vital, but too often they neglect it. They become so busy maintaining church life that nobody thinks much about evangelism. By initiating an outreach program and giving it high priority, you will regularly add new believers to your congregation. And your people will be equipped and excited about evangelism.

The most effective way to reach people is *through people.* Church newspaper ads, mailed flyers, knocking on doors—none of these things are as effective as people in the local church reaching out to their friends and families.

Consider initiating an evangelistic coffee hour for women.

Two couples could begin an outreach-oriented home Bible study for couples. The men of your church might begin a men's breakfast with the goal of inviting friends and business associates to share Christ with them. Organize evangelistic suppers or special banquets where each person brings a friend. Invite a good speaker. Plan a relaxing, friendly evening during which the gospel is presented clearly. Be creative!

Growing congregations reach out to their communities. How is your group reaching out? Is it effective? Are people coming to Christ through the individual and corporate witness of your church?

Each church needs a growth program to keep it eagerly praying and evangelizing. Coupled with this, the church needs a growth climate (as discussed in chapter six). Excitement is contagious! And excitement is an excellent climate for growth. If your congregation gets excited about what God is doing in your church, they will bring friends and family to a service. Then you can follow up these contacts through your growth program.

Assimilate Newcomers into Your Group

Every church has an "in" group. If you don't realize this, you're probably in it. In many churches it takes people five years or more to enter this core group. Many people who have attended for six months or a year leave because they continue to be excluded. They lament, "We never felt at home" or, "We were never fully accepted."

A young couple who recently began attending a new church related the following story:

> We went to the young adult Sunday school class which consisted of about ten couples. After class, at least one

> partner from each of those couples told us, "It's so good to have you here. We hope you come back next week." Of course, we couldn't help but return to that church. We didn't receive just the usual greeter-at-the-door welcome. Instead, the entire Sunday school class had welcomed us warmly. That made all the difference to us!

The welcome was genuine, and this couple continued attending. They were assimilated and brought into the "in" group.

Some churches welcome people the first Sunday they visit, but no other interaction ever takes place. Newcomers are not challenged to get involved in the church. Eventually they begin attending some other church where they are not only warmly welcomed, but also encouraged to be an active part of the "family."

Open up your inner circle. Learn to involve people through small groups—choirs, home Bible studies, and the teamwork of children's and youth programs. Allow people who have trusted Christ to use their gifts and feel wanted in your church.

Small groups open the front door by making people feel welcome, and they close the back door by getting them involved. New people will stay when they feel they're a part of the group.

Encourage Spiritual Gifts

A growing church encourages its people to exercise their spiritual gifts. Romans 12, 1 Corinthians 12, Ephesians 4, and 1 Peter 4 emphasize the importance of the spiritual gifts God has given his church. Each of these passages challenges believers to *use* these gifts from God.

Scripture clearly emphasizes that ministry is for everyone—not just for designated church leaders. Are you using the spiritual gifts of each member of your congregation? Unfortunately the church often fails to teach, encourage, and provide opportunities for its members to use their spiritual gifts.

First, a growing church teaches about spiritual gifts. In the last three years, has your congregation studied spiritual gifts? How many in your fellowship can identify their spiritual gifts? Do they know how to use these gifts?

Second, a growing church encourages people to discover their gifts. Leaders should help others identify their gifts and use those gifts for God. You can encourage someone who is using his spiritual gift by specifically identifying the gift and thanking him for using it.

Third, a growing church provides ample opportunities for people to use their gifts. Their aim is to help each Christian use his or her gifts in the most appropriate area of need.

The New Testament lists at least twenty gifts that God has given to the church. Some churches place great emphasis on the "sign" gifts. Other churches push the "pulpit" gifts of teaching and preaching. Sometimes those are the only gifts that are identified, encouraged, and developed.

But Christ has generously given *many* spiritual gifts to each local church. Encourage Christians to develop all of their spiritual gifts. How desperately the body of Christ needs those with the gift of encouragement to lift up the easily discouraged! How urgently we need to challenge those gifted in administration to help organize our confused programs. How many would be comforted if those with the gift of mercy were using their gift fully? If a church desires to grow, it must encourage each individual to put his gifts to work.

Many of today's churches need to release women to use their gifts. Too many of our churches imply that women are gifted only in the nursery, kitchen, or Sunday school. Some women may be gifted speakers or small group Bible study leaders. We must recognize and affirm that women are just as gifted and talented as men. Leaders should actively help women, as well as men, develop and use their gifts fully.

Leaders in various churches differ in interpreting Scripture passages which mention the role of women in the church. Frequently mentioned passages include 1 Corinthians 11 and 14, and 1 Timothy 2. Many other passages also speak to this question. Each local fellowship has the freedom and obligation to do what it believes is biblical. But even those with a traditional view of the role of women in the church should recognize the great need for women to exercise their gifts within the body of believers. Commit yourself to encouraging these gifted women.

How grateful I am for the women using their gifts in our church family! This morning several of our women with the gift of teaching taught the Bible to small groups of women. Yesterday I conferred with one of our women who regularly counsels a young couple who struggles with a difficult marriage. Last night I spoke long distance with a woman who is helping a new Christian find an evangelical church in his town. To reach the goal of growth, the church body must use the gifts of each person in its fellowship, both male and female.

The New Testament teaches that God has given many gifts, all of which are to be used for his glory. We must recognize that men and women are *equally* gifted. When each gift is properly used, the church can become all God meant it to be.

Expect Excellence

Growth requires a commitment to excellence, so encourage your congregation toward that goal. Too often we settle for far less than the best. Healthy, growing churches are continually improving. A group that wants to grow says, "We *can* do better. We *will* do better in the future."

Growth naturally requires a holy dissatisfaction—a sense

of wanting to be better for God. Growing churches aren't satisfied with mediocrity, but continually encourage improvement in their song leaders, Sunday school teachers, youth leaders, and preachers. The growing congregation seeks and expects excellence.

But if your fellowship believes "any effort is fine as long as you love the Lord," it's likely that you won't see growth. As we said before, this attitude is often an excuse for laziness or poor quality from a less-than-best effort.

Church leaders can learn to evaluate, encourage, and challenge their people to excellence. Some people will drag their feet every step of the way. However, most will be delighted by the help and encouragement offered. They will be refreshed with the challenge to grow and improve.

Is your desire that every part of your congregation strive for excellence for the glory of God? Then each member should strive individually to be the best he can, to serve God wholeheartedly and with all his energy—to hold his own match to the coals of church growth.

In the book *McDonalds: Behind the Arches,* author John F. Love examines the phenomenal success of this fast-food chain. He quotes the company's chairman: "We were continually looking for a better way to do things, and then a revised better way to do things, and then a revised, revised better way."

With such an attitude is it any wonder that McDonalds has done so well? Surely Christians, the stewards of God's great news, should be committed to excellence as well. We ought to strive for excellence in our individual lives and in our life together as a church body.

Scripture itself encourages us to do our best for God: "And whatever you do, whether in word or deed, do it all in the name of the Lord Jesus, giving thanks to God the Father through Him" (Col. 3:17).

Emphasize Quality Preaching

The congregation that plans to grow also strives for excellence in preaching. Studies of growing churches report that pulpit ministry is a major factor in church growth. If a growing local church only has one person doing all the preaching, that church finds the best preacher available.

However, in some churches, the pulpit ministry may be shared by five to twenty-five leaders in the course of a year. Thus, attaining quality preaching becomes quite a challenge. If every man in a church is extended the opportunity to preach—which suggests that this church is not primarily concerned about the quality of what is said from the pulpit—then that congregation probably will not grow.

Christians today are accustomed to great preaching. They hear it on Christian radio and television stations and on audio tapes of popular preachers. It should not surprise us that they expect to hear quality preaching in their churches. Many unbelievers hear excellent speakers at clubs and business seminars. Why should they listen attentively to someone who stumbles over his own words from behind a pulpit?

Although local churches usually can't provide the caliber of a Charles Swindoll or a John MacArthur week after week, they can strive for the best preaching possible. The growing church doesn't allow everyone to preach. Rather, it encourages the two, three, or four leaders who are the most gifted preachers to develop and use their gift extensively.

A congregation short of good preachers should look outside to gifted men for help, but they should not be satisfied with a different preacher each week. Scheduling the same preacher for three, four, or more consecutive weeks provides continuity from the pulpit.

Some of you may be thinking, "I enjoy our variety of

preachers—from young Tom to old Mr. Jones." I challenge you to re-examine your personal preference with church growth eyes. Variety in preaching may tickle the spiritual tastebuds while giving many a chance to speak. But does it provide good food for hungry visitors or recognize God's teaching about spiritual gifts?

If you've attended the same congregation for fifteen years and you're grounded in the Word, you may be comfortable with the present quality of preaching. You know and love that preacher, even if he isn't a particularly gifted public speaker.

But if you want your church to grow, if you expect people to come to stay, you must listen with visitor's ears. Visitors won't say, "That was a terrible message, but he's such a loving preacher." They will simply find a church with consistently strong preaching. A new Christian or visitor doesn't evaluate a sermon by who the preacher is, but rather by what he hears.

A few churches have grown without evangelistic efforts or good preaching. But two characteristics of most growing churches are consistent, life-changing preaching and a strong emphasis on reaching both inside and outside the church body for growth. It may take a lot of time and energy to get your church growth fires burning, but it will be worth it when you benefit from the steady light and warmth and see the increasing flame.

Study Questions

1. "Churches know evangelism is vital, but too often they

neglect it." Does your congregation have a specific growth program? What new evangelistic outreaches could your congregation initiate?

2. "New people will stay when they feel they're a part of the group." Of the last ten adults who visited your congregation at least twice, how many have been assimilated? How might you more effectively encourage new people to take an active part in your fellowship?

3. "Scripture clearly emphasizes that ministry is for everyone." How many people in your congregation can identify their spiritual gifts? How could you encourage others to discover and use their gifts for God?

4. "Growth requires a holy dissatisfaction—a sense of wanting to be better for God." In what areas do you want to see your congregation improve? What would it take to strive for excellence in these areas?

5. "One characteristic of most growing churches is consistent, life-changing preaching." What caliber of preaching does your church provide from week to week right now? How might your congregation develop a more consistent, quality preaching ministry?

8

The Church Growth Yardstick

WHEN YOU WERE A CHILD, did your mother stand you up beside the family yardstick and measure how much taller you'd grown? Every year when you surpassed the pencil lines of the year before, it felt like a great, personal achievement.

Measuring church growth isn't quite as easy as that. But measuring is possible, and it is important. Churches grow numerically in four basic ways.

Biological growth occurs when babies born to church families grow up and remain in the fellowship. Even if your church grows only through these families where parents teach their faith in Christ to their children, then it should be growing.

We should pray and work to see our children come to

Christ. The responsibility and privilege belongs both to parents and to the church family. But although biological growth is important, it does not fulfill the Great Commission.

Transfer growth occurs when a Christian family from another area moves into your neighborhood and joins your fellowship. If your congregation is located in a growing city or county, you may grow numerically without doing any outreach at all.

Sometimes churches grow because they attract members from other churches in the community. But whether believers transfer from a local church or from another area, transfer growth is not fulfilling the Great Commission either. We must not confuse real growth—seeing people receive Christ—with the geographic relocation of believers.

Wake-up growth occurs when believers who have nominal church ties and who have slipped away from a walk with Christ recommit themselves to Christ and to fellowship. Reaching the sidetracked Christian is growth that counts. If you spiritually awaken these people and bring them into your congregation, you extend God's kingdom by gathering Christians who will be taught and discipled for Christ.

Conversion growth. The types of growth discussed above are good, but conversion growth—the winning of lost souls to Jesus Christ—must be a primary aim. Christians must have a vision of reaching unbelievers with the gospel. *If you aren't concerned about conversion growth, you have lost God's perspective.*

In my first years at Palm Bible Chapel in Florida, we quickly grew numerically. One year our average Sunday morning attendance increased from less than 200 to more than 300. Approximately ten adults were born again that first year, but most of our growth was transfer growth. In the following years, our numerical growth was much slower, but an increased number were putting their faith in Jesus Christ.

Although conversion growth comes slowly, it is eternally significant. In conversion growth, people are born again, enter fellowship, and become disciples of Christ. If you want your church to grow, you cannot be satisfied with anything less than conversion growth.

Often churches which are growing due to biological, transfer or wake-up growth become self-satisfied when they should be humbly striving for conversion growth. But for today's churches, significant conversion growth should be a *primary* goal.

Keeping Track

How can you know if your fellowship is growing? Good attendance records will help you recognize various forms of growth. They also help distinguish real growth from wishful thinking. Good statistics help the leadership team understand what takes place in the church.

Some people react against keeping records and statistics. Perhaps you formerly attended a church which misused numbers. The leaders were satisfied only if their numbers were larger than last year's or better than another church's with which they competed. This kind of church keeps statistics in order to boast and often places more importance on numbers than the people they represent. In some churches numbers do become more important than people. But potential negatives should not hinder you from the many benefits of keeping accurate records.

Numbers Represent People

Statistics are important because they represent individuals. Suppose someone tells you, "At the beach I saw ten people get into a boat built for six. None of them wore lifejackets.

When they had gone about 200 yards, one of the men stood to shift his position, capsizing the boat and throwing all ten people overboard. Fortunately, my friend and I saw them, raced to them in our boat, and saved some of them."

Immediately you ask him, "How many did you save?"

He replies, "Well, I really don't pay attention to numbers. Does it matter? We saved some of them."

"But how many did you save?" you ask more urgently.

He replies, "I think we saved at least two, probably three."

"What about the other seven?" you ask.

"I don't know," the man says, "but the three we saved, we saved well."

Three were saved, but seven drowned. Statistics *do* matter! Numbers especially count before God. Each person who is not born again through your congregation's witness this year is one person who is lost for eternity if he isn't reached in time. For years some local churches have excused, justified, and defended their lack of effective outreach by saying that numbers don't count. This attitude should make us weep!

When we count the number who hear the Word preached on Sunday morning or the number who profess Christ during one year, we do it because those numbers represent individuals—people who matter to God.

Numbers Help in Planning

If you keep accurate statistics, you can plan better for the future.

When our congregation in Florida decided to have its first-ever Christmas Eve service, we didn't know how many people to expect. About ninety people thought it was a good idea, so I estimated that approximately fifty would attend. Imagine my surprise when 120 people attended! How did I know it was 120 people? Because we kept records. Why? So that next year we could avoid some of the crowding problems we experienced that first year.

We didn't plan for ushers because we thought the fifty people who came could seat themselves. We wanted everyone to sit in a certain part of the 340-seat auditorium. As people streamed in, I realized that we should have planned for ushers.

We also neglected to plan for a nursery. Fifty people might bring three to five babies. No problem. But 120 people brought thirteen babies. Major panic! Instead of enjoying the Christmas Eve service, my wife and daughter served as the emergency nursery crew. Statistics do help in planning.

Accurate records also provide an objective guideline when changes are proposed. Consider what happens if you don't keep records and someone proposes enlarging the nursery. Although you know the capacity of the nursery, no one knows the average number of children in the nursery each Sunday. Accurate statistics distinguish legitimate needs from personal whims. A congregation needs accurate records to improve planning and preparation.

Numbers Help in Evaluation

Statistics also help in evaluation, especially in evaluating attendance.

In our assembly in Alberta we didn't keep attendance records consistently. For a few years we kept statistics, but then we neglected it for awhile. When we weren't keeping records, our leaders would debate about whether we were growing. No one knew for certain! If we had kept statistics, we would have known. Keeping accurate statistics prevents time wasted speculating. You can evaluate on the basis of facts. The facts eliminate confusion.

Design an attendance form, designate a reliable attendance keeper, and begin keeping accurate attendance records beginning next Sunday morning. The leaders of your church should evaluate these statistics at least quarterly.

Numbers Help Determine Growth Goals

Record keeping will also help you set good growth goals. Remember the ancient proverb: "He that aimeth at nothing shall surely hit it."

A missionary to Latin America and I spent several days together recently sharing our visions, dreams, and hopes. How encouraging it was to hear him discuss the growth God had given his ministry during the past five years! It was even more exciting to hear him share the numerical growth goals he had already set for the next five years.

To help your church grow, keep accurate statistics and prayerfully evaluate what God can and wants to do through you. Then, in faith, set goals toward which you will pray and work. Periodically evaluate your goals to determine if you are on target.

Have you set a measurable growth goal in your particular area of ministry—whether it's a Sunday school class, youth group, or Bible study? Prayerfully set a growth goal for the coming year for your ministry area. This goal will challenge and encourage both you and your co-workers.

If you teach Sunday school, what is the average attendance for your class? Compared to last year, has attendance gone up or down? You may say, "My attendance averages five—the same five kids every Sunday."

Don't settle for that. Even if your church isn't growing, your Sunday school class can grow. Attempt to average at least six students before year's end. Determine to increase attendance to nine by the following year. If you plan and work creatively, you can do it with God's help.

Plan, evaluate, and set goals according to your accurate

statistics. Then when your congregation does grow, you can rejoice, knowing that each number represents an individual whom God loves very much.

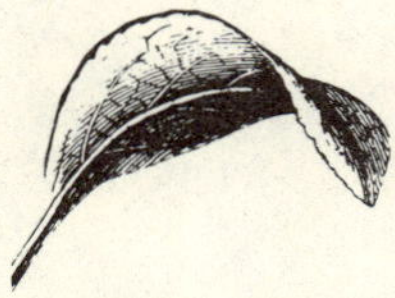

Study Questions

1. "Churches grow numerically in four basic ways." How much have each of these ways contributed to your congregation's growth in recent years?

2. "Conversion growth—the winning of lost souls to Jesus Christ—must be a primary aim." In what ways does your congregation strive for significant conversion growth? What would it take for this to be your primary aim?

3. "Numbers represent individuals—people who are important to God." Does your church have attendance records on all meetings and events for the last three years? In what specific ways could you begin keeping or using attendance records more effectively?

III

The Cost of Growth

9

But Who's Leading?

We the willing, led by the unknowing,
Are doing the impossible for the ungrateful.
We have done so much, for so long, for so little,
We are qualified to do anything, for nothing, forever.

THIS SAYING SUGGESTS a great deal of hard work and confusion. Obviously, being a leader is not synonymous with being popular or comfortable! Yet throughout history God has worked through key leaders like Moses and Joshua, Deborah and Gideon, David and Solomon, Nehemiah and Zerubbabel, and Peter and Paul. It's not surprising that where God grows a strong local church, he uses strong leaders.

E. M. Bounds said, "The Church is looking for better methods; God is looking for better men."

Peter Wagner, a noted authority on church growth, emphasizes strong leadership as a common denominator in growing churches. A growing church has leaders who are committed to growth. They want their church to grow and are willing to pay the price of growth.

Many leaders would rather relinquish their responsibility for growth—or lack of it—in their church. It's easier to pass the responsibility to the congregation, the community, or the Holy Spirit.

When challenged with the responsibility of leading their churches to growth, some leaders feel like a certain star runner of a college football team. His team was losing an important game to a bigger, stronger, faster team. Every time he carried the ball he was battered, bruised, and thrown for a loss. By halftime, he felt exhausted and discouraged.

In the third quarter, the home crowd noticed that the quarterback wasn't giving the ball to him anymore. They watched in dismay as the ball was handed to one runner who lost four yards and another who lost ten. The frustrated home crowd began chanting the runner's name. To their surprise and confusion, the quarterback turned to them, lifted his hands to quiet the crowd, and shouted, "He doesn't want the ball!"

Like that fullback, church leaders sometimes want to step out of the spotlight and let someone else carry the ball. But leaders must accept this responsibility if their churches are to grow.

1 Timothy 3, Titus 1, and 1 Peter 5 list several qualities shared by God's leaders. Each of these passages encourages two vital skills: paying attention to people and providing direction for people.

Pay Attention to People

Leaders need to become more people-oriented. They are often capable managers of finances, administration, and building renovations, but sometimes weak in relating to people. The leader who pays attention to people—the man who leads a church to growth—has the following qualities:

1. *He has a servant's attitude.* Successful managers in business have discovered the importance of leaders with a serving attitude. The April 1986 issue of *Inc.* reports: "The leader's role is to create vision . . . The role of the leader is a servant's role. It's supporting his people, running interference for them. It's coming out with an atmosphere of understanding and trust—and love."

   Is your local church led by servant-minded Christians? Jesus said, "The greatest among you should be like the youngest, and the one who rules like the one who serves. For who is greater, the one who is at the table or the one who serves? Is it not the one who is at the table? But I am among you as one who serves" (Luke 22:26-27).

   A church leader should not be a domineering, power-hungry dictator who barks orders to God's people. Rather, he should approach leadership as an opportunity to serve God's people, to lay down his life for them. The Bible instructs these leaders: "Be shepherds of God's flock that is under your care, serving as overseers—not because you must, but because you are willing, as God wants you to be; not greedy for money, but eager to serve; not lording it over those entrusted to you, but being examples to the flock" (1 Peter 5:2-3).

2. *He is a good role model.* The apostle Paul wrote, "Follow my example, as I follow the example of Christ" (1 Cor. 11:1). What a risky suggestion! Yet the New Testament clearly states that not only Paul, but all leaders should be role models of what others in the church are to become.

   Paul also wrote, "Join with others in following my

example, brothers, and take note of those who live according to the pattern we gave you" (Phil. 3:17). Paul wasn't placing himself on a pedestal. A few verses earlier he humbly confessed that he certainly hadn't "arrived" as a Christian (Phil. 3:12). Yet he was a good example as a leader.

Educators have carefully analyzed what the apostle Paul instinctively knew: People follow models. To Timothy, Paul writes, "Don't let anyone look down on you because you are young, but set an example for the believers in speech, in life, in love, in faith and in purity" (1 Tim. 4:12).

Does your church leadership provide good models? Do older men and women provide a model of Christian commitment, excitement about reaching the lost, and dedication to church growth? Do the attitudes and lifestyles of leaders provide models for the rest of the congregation?

Hebrews 13:7 teaches, "Remember your leaders, who spoke the word of God to you. Consider the outcome of their way of life and imitate their faith."

3. *He demonstrates concern for others.* I have never met a church leader who wasn't concerned about the people in his church, but I have met many who didn't communicate this love and concern to their congregations. Preachers and elders sometimes seem aloof, removed, or uncaring. Their lack of time, effort, or understanding of communication makes these leaders seem distant and unaware of problems. How would people in your church respond when asked, "Do your leaders really care about you?"

The apostle Paul reminds the Christians in Thessalonica that he had been among them "like a mother caring for her little children" and "as a father deals with his own children" (1 Thess. 2:7, 11). The Thessalonians experienced and sensed Paul's love for them.

The best-sellers *In Search of Excellence* and *The Pursuit of Excellence* emphasize a people-management principle called M.B.W.A.—Management By Walking Around. This principle challenges corporate executives to spend time with their employees, asking questions and listening carefully to their needs and feelings. Should local church leaders do less for God's people?

As a member of your local congregation, how do you make others feel appreciated? How often do you thank or compliment those serving in Sunday school, youth ministries, or music? Do fellow Christians hear, see, and feel your appreciation? I'm grieved when someone says of me, "That man never smiles at me. He doesn't care what I think. None of our elders have ever encouraged me." The leaders and each member in your church should actively care for people.

4. *He has the ability to communicate well.* It doesn't take newlyweds long to realize that communication is a vital factor in a successful marriage. Likewise, church leaders must realize that communication is essential in a growing congregation.

Good leaders are good communicators. The Pursuit of Excellence quotes Admiral Zumwalt on how to command a ship: "What I tried hardest to do was ensure that every officer and man on the ship not only knew what we were about . . . but also managed to understand enough about how it all fitted together that he could begin to experience some of the fun and challenge that those of us in the top slots were having . . . More important . . . was the basic effort to communicate a sense of excitement, fun, and zest in all that we were doing."

Good shepherds use every means possible to keep the congregation informed so that each person feels a part of the church. This flow of information includes congregational meetings, financial reports, newsletters, telephone calls, and home visits. Leaders need to ask questions, heed the advice of others, and share information.

Leaders Provide Direction for People

Is your church being shaped like a sand dune or a sculpture? Sand dunes are formed by the varying influences of wind and water. In many local churches, decisions are made and changes implemented with no grasp of what ultimate form the church should take. The church may desire to be a New Testament church, but it's shaped by the consensus of the congregation or the strong reaction of a few—the varying influences that result in a sand pile.

In contrast, a sculpture is purposely formed by a sculptor who has in his mind a clear picture of the finished work. With this goal, the artist gradually molds the raw material into a specific shape.

Church leaders, on their knees with the Bible in their hands, should decide what shape their churches could become by the grace of God. They must study the Bible, the needs of their people, and the needs of their community. Then with sensitivity and purpose these leaders can guide their churches through change to growth.

Growing churches recognize that everyone in a position of authority may not have the God-given gift of leadership. Although each should have a pastor's heart and the characteristics described in 1 Timothy 3, Titus 1, and 1 Peter 5, the gift of leadership mentioned in Romans 12:8 is not given to all.

Each church must allow its gifted leaders to lead. In every church, two or three people have more vision and God-given leadership ability than others. These few may or may not be the designated leaders. But the church must encourage these gifted leaders to lead.

Churches have lost many frustrated people who were not given an opportunity to use their God-given leadership talents. Eager to serve, full of ideas, and gifted by God, they faced too many roadblocks in their congregations and are leading in other churches or para-church organizations today. In many cases the fellowships they left behind continue to flounder because the church cannot provide necessary leadership.

Those who lead a church to growth must provide direction. The following five qualities are characteristic of such leaders:

1. *A leader has vision.* A growing church needs at least one individual with vision and expectant faith. All Christians expect that God will do great things—somewhere, sometime, through someone. But church growth leaders believe that God is going to do something great—here, now, through us!

   Church leaders should envision what kind of church they can become by God's grace. This vision must be based on a solid understanding of where the church needs to grow and how the various parts fit together. A leader should communicate this vision to the rest of the congregation. Leaders help others in the local church grow and dream in expectant faith.

2. *A leader takes decisive action.* It's easier to talk about what should be done than to accomplish it. Elders and

deacons often theorize or discuss practical steps, but then indefinitely postpone taking steps of action.

Committed people gifted in leadership don't settle for discussion and prayer without corresponding action. They lead in making and implementing decisions. Every group needs a member who, after each discussion, consistently asks, "*Who* will do it? *How* will it be done? *What* is our target date?"

Anyone can theorize and criticize, but leaders act decisively. Theodore Roosevelt said, "Far better it is to dare mighty things, to win glorious triumphs even though checkered by failure, than to rank with those poor spirits who neither enjoy nor suffer much because they live in the gray twilight that knows neither victory nor defeat."

How many growth ideas have your elders discussed with no results? Where is the leader—or team of leaders—who will take decisive action? As someone wisely put it, "Even if you're on the right track, you'll get run over if you just sit there."

3. *A leader rebounds quickly.* Because leaders are human, they make mistakes, fail, and receive criticism. Cultivate the perspective of Winston Churchill, Britain's Prime Minister, during World War II. After presenting a gloomy war report to his Cabinet, he lit a cigar, smiled, and said, "Gentlemen, I find it rather inspiring." What a leadership attitude! Churchill also said, "Nothing in life is so exhilarating as to be shot at—without result."

People who don't have the gift of leadership may feel easily defeated. Facing one critical report or voiced opposition, they prepare to abandon ship. I have been criticized to my face and behind my back. I didn't enjoy either, but I learned from both. Expect criticism, for it will surely come.

But don't allow criticism to anger or depress you. Bounce back quickly from mistakes, failures, and criticism. As you struggle with doubts or pain, try to project enthusiasm and optimism. Keep your eyes on God, and remember that the only opinion that truly counts is his (1 Cor. 4:1-5).

4. *A leader motivates others.* Church leaders regularly bemoan the lack of committed people willing to volunteer to serve in their churches. And although it does seem that a handful of energetic servers handle the majority of the work load, don't waste time pointing fingers and blaming others.

   Take the responsibility to recruit, train, encourage, and, above all, motivate people. Someone once said, "A gifted leader is someone who not only motivates people to do what they don't want to do, but also gets them to enjoy doing it." Many Christians want to serve God, but require leaders to motivate them into service.

   Sensitive, effective leaders learn to share their vision, to encourage people, to make them feel wanted and needed. Effective leaders motivate by helping people feel that they are an important element of the team. As a part of your local congregation, ask yourself: "How can I motivate people toward service for God and church growth?"

5. *A leader innovates regularly.* Leading a church to growth includes leading it to change. Prepare for change and encourage change wherever it is needed. Remember—gifted leaders are innovators!

Why Some Fear Change

In general, most people are wary of change. And this is also true of some Christians in the church—especially when it comes to the issue of church growth. It helps to acknowledge this fear, which may be caused by some of these factors:

1. *Age.* As people grow older they increasingly enjoy the routine and may feel inclined to resist change. If you find yourself continually resisting change in your local church, perhaps it's time to step aside and allow younger people to lead the congregation through the changes needed during the years ahead.

2. *Personality.* Perhaps God gave you a pastoral heart and has developed godly character in you, but he never gave you the gift of leadership. Then allow others to lead. If you truly put God's kingdom first, you won't fight change, but will embrace it graciously.

3. *A sincere desire to be true to God's Word.* Resist change that moves your church away from the Bible. The truth we preach must never change. But don't resist needed change by justifying traditions with Bible verses. Through its silence on these subjects, the New Testament allows tremendous latitude in meeting and organizational structure, musical style and types of outreach.

4. *A natural fear of criticism.* Perhaps we fear the criticism of another local church, a preacher, or a significant traditional person in the church, or even what someone who used to be in the church would say if he saw what we're now doing. We should admit this fear to God and

pray for courage to do what is biblically best for the health and growth of the church.

5. *A busy schedule,* which will become only busier if change is implemented. Don't allow fear of discomfort—of being stretched—to keep you from leading to change. Embrace change and lead the way. Why should so many young adults in our churches see their leaders as roadblocks to change? Those who want to do something for God are prepared to follow through with action. But they need leaders who will encourage their efforts and lead the way in required change.

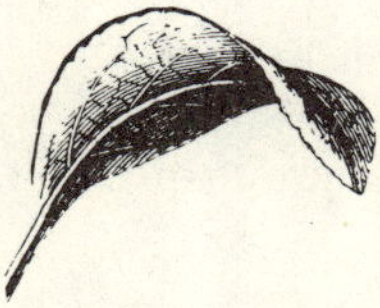

Study Questions

1. "Where God grows a strong local church, he uses strong leaders." What discourages some from being strong leaders?

2. "Leaders pay attention to people." In what ways do you consciously do this already? In what ways could you pay better attention to others?

3. "Leaders provide direction for people." In your mind, what shape is your congregation taking? Is it more like a sand dune or a sculpture? Which leaders are exerting the most influence in this process of change?

4. "The local church must allow its gifted leaders to lead." What qualities characterize gifted leaders? Who would you identify as the five most gifted leaders within your congregation?

5. "Some Christians fear change." What factors may cause leaders or other individuals in your church to fear change? How important is it to admit and overcome this fear?

10

What Will It Cost? . . .

LIFE ALWAYS INVOLVES compromise. I love ice cream, but I also wish to keep my thirty-three-inch waist. The more I enjoy the one, the less I enjoy the other. So I find a happy medium, sometimes sacrificing ice cream and sometimes enjoying it thoroughly.

I enjoy a comfortable church atmosphere where everyone knows everyone else, everyone agrees on issues, and everyone does the same things together each week. But I also realize that God wants us to reach the world for Christ—he wants our churches to grow. And we can't always have both a comfortable church and a growing church.

Church growth requires commitment and sacrifice. Your

church won't make that sacrifice unless its members commit themselves to reaching people for Christ and integrating them into the church body.

Jesus challenged those interested in following him to count the cost. Local churches must likewise count the cost of growing for his glory. Although they would never admit it, some congregations aren't willing to pay that price. The high price of growth prevents many churches from growing. Let me suggest some costs your church must count if it is going to grow.

Making Changes

Growing congregations have people who are willing to pay the price of change. Recognize that all growth involves change. You cannot grow and remain the same.

But change is difficult for all of us. Many of us can identify with the person who said, "Any change, at any time, in any way, for any reason, is bad." Such a reaction is natural, but not very spiritual.

Acts 6 describes a church that had to change as it grew. The apostles couldn't properly administer the distribution of food to the widows and still give adequate time to Scripture and prayer. This leadership and delegation problem demanded new procedures. The fellowship appointed seven men to supervise that distribution. I suspect that some people resisted this change.

Changes are not easy to accept. If the leaders of a church decide to change from one central prayer meeting to several home groups, they may receive criticism. People who have attended the prayer meeting in the past may decide to cast their vote of disapproval by not attending. Sadly, some Christians demonstrate their spiritual immaturity with that kind of attitude.

Some older Christians find change particularly difficult. Even minor changes like using a new hymnbook can be difficult for those who have sung from the same book for forty years. But that old hymnbook could be completely inadequate for the congregation's new and younger Christians. Although singing from a newer songbook may be a painful change for some older Christians, this change might attract more younger people. Growth necessarily involves change—sometimes subtle change, like new hymnbooks, but other times a more dramatic change is required.

Church growth studies indicate that in a typical congregation about two percent of the people are innovators who want change continually (sometimes for no good reason!). Fifteen percent listen to the innovators, are prepared to change, and lead in the change. Another seventy percent are willing to go along with the change. And ten to fifteen percent never support any change.

The growing church should be sensitive to that resistant fifteen percent, but should not allow them to hinder growth. Don't place too much emphasis on the negative votes. Some people react negatively to almost every change. If you wait until everyone agrees with the change, you will not grow. I heartily believe in biblical unity. But if leaders allow two or three tradition-bound people to dictate their opinions to the rest of the congregation, the church's growth will be stunted.

Moving ahead in spite of complaints is especially difficult when you know, love, and have worked with those who resist change. Moving ahead requires strong leaders who listen to others, communicate well, and pray often. These leaders must have the courage to make changes they believe are necessary for the good of the church and for growth.

Changes are inevitable in the human body, in families, in businesses, and in cities and countries. Growth will bring changes in the church, too. Are you prepared for the discomfort caused by that change?

Training and Equipping

Because adequate training is essential for growth, growing churches commit themselves to training and equipping believers for ministry. Training requires an investment of time and effort, but if we believe Ephesians 4:11-12 and are challenged by 2 Timothy 2:2, we will set our minds to preparing people to effect church growth.

Training is especially important in fellowships which don't rely heavily on seminary-trained professionals. Ordinary Christians, not clergy, are expected to do the ministry. But often these very fellowships fail to train their own people! Congregations determined to pay the price of growth invest time, effort, and money into training individuals to minister. Song leaders, preachers, Sunday school teachers, visitation people, and those who evangelize can all benefit from practical training. We must motivate those currently involved in ministries to train others to serve in their ministry areas.

Some leaders are unable to train others. Maybe they learned by trial and error because no one took time to train them. Fortunately a multitude of training resources are available—counseling seminars, Sunday school conventions, evangelism workshops, and other training available through books, audio cassettes, and video tapes. Smaller congregations can ask larger churches to share resource people to train their people in areas where they need outside help.

I believe that God holds us responsible for neglecting the excellent training resources available and remaining in a static pattern of repeating our mistakes. Is your church committed to training and equipping the saints?

Using Gifted People

Ministry in biblical churches is not based on professional status, but on spiritual gifts. Churches need to put those gifted members to work! Your church should be ready to train and equip the people the Holy Spirit wants to use. Provide gifted people with opportunities to develop and use their God-given gifts; the result is growth in quality and quantity.

Growing congregations have leaders who take the initiative, who develop and utilize the gifts of the entire fellowship. These people should approach others with certain spiritual gifts and encourage them to use those gifts in the church. Ask new people and new Christians to use their gifts. Each person should feel a vital part of your church.

Sometimes we have to ask someone to stop using what they think is his gift, but isn't. No one enjoys this painful task. Yet a growing church must learn to say, "Brother, you do a great job in visitation. But you can't lead the singing anymore. Please consider involvement in visitation and let one of the others lead the singing." Or, "We're grateful that you've served as Sunday school superintendent for the last ten years. But we think it's time you give someone else an opportunity to direct that ministry." Confrontation is costly and difficult. But those who can deal graciously, yet firmly, must speak up when someone is involved in an area for which he is obviously not gifted.

Sometimes sincere Christians minister in an area where they are not gifted only because no one has offered to replace them. Years ago in a local church, we wanted to encourage our younger adults to teach Sunday school. Many people feared that our veteran teaching staff, whose average age was sixty, wouldn't step aside graciously. But as the congregation grew and younger people expressed interest in teaching, three of the older teachers asked to step aside to allow young men and women to teach. These older people didn't resist the change, but were delighted to allow others to serve.

Be prepared to step aside yourself and also to encourage others to step aside.

Spending Money

Growth has financial costs, too. Some churches may feel this is the biggest roadblock to change if they are on a limited budget. But if we believe that God will provide the growth, we can also believe that he will provide the money.

Some churches don't grow simply because even if they have the money, they are too reluctant to spend it. If we are afraid to spend $150 for a new sign, the outer appearance of our church will continue to look shabby. That faded sign announces to the world: "We don't care." A passer-by might reason, "If they don't care about their facilities, they probably won't be interested in me." This is an excellent way to lose potential visitors! Is it worth the cost to you?

Perhaps at a business meeting someone might suggest, "We should renovate our Sunday school classrooms. They're dark and unappealing." Someone else may immediately respond, "Where will we get the money?" Another might add, "That money should go to missions." Who can argue against missions? So the Sunday school environment continues to look shabby and uninviting. Sensitive parents attend church where their children enjoy Sunday school. The decision to neglect the Sunday school classrooms can be very costly in terms of loss of potential growth.

If your church always tries to save money, it's likely you are not growing. Growth costs money. A larger church means purchasing more Sunday school materials, more training, more equipment, and maybe even some paint for those Sunday school classrooms.

Perhaps the congregation should contribute so young members can attend an important training seminar. If the leadership truly wants people to become better equipped for ministry, they will designate some money for training and equipping. Growth costs money. Your members will put their money where their commitment lies.

When your church begins to grow, you may need a new building or an extra lot for additional parking. Don't let these costs scare you. As congregations grow, income grows too. People become enthusiastic about giving when they see their fellowship growing. And there are more members to share those costs.

Investing More Time

Growth also requires an additional investment of time. You may be surprised to discover how much time you need to invest in a growing church.

As a group begins to grow, the leaders necessarily spend more time in prayer and evaluation. Planning programs and equipping people require increased effort. More people are doing more things—that requires some complex coordination of the various roles and responsibilities. Every area of church life becomes more time consuming.

Communication also requires more time. As a church adds to its numbers, its leaders must communicate with the congregation more and more effectively. Healthy communication seems difficult enough in a small group. It becomes even more difficult in a larger congregation.

If growth has begun but no one is willing to invest time in visiting and assimilating new people, then growth will not continue. When leaders don't invest time in organizing, visiting, and telephoning, they stop the growth process.

Sometimes people need to reconsider their priorities. Perhaps they devote too much time and energy to community activities or para-church organizations. I am saddened that some of our local churches produce no growth, yet they volunteer many hours to various Christian organizations and groups.

If you want your church to grow, you have to invest more time. Although your schedule already may be full, the additional time you invest will certainly be worthwhile. You may need to take a look at your priority list and do some rearranging.

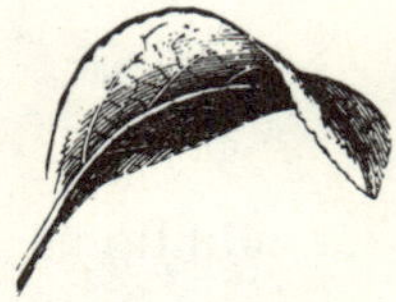

Study Questions

1. "We can't always have both a comfortable church and a growing church." What conditions cause us to prefer comfort over growth? What makes growth worth the discomfort it creates?

2. "Local churches must likewise count the cost of growing for his glory." Of the five costs mentioned in this chapter, which cost seems most uncomfortable to you?

3. "Growing congregations have people who are willing to pay the price of change." Do you tend to innovate, lead, go along with, or initially resist change?

4. "Growing churches commit themselves to training and equipping believers for ministry." How were you equipped for ministry within your congregation? What additional training opportunities might you and others benefit from?

5. "Growing congregations have leaders who take the initiative, who develop and utilize the gifts of the entire fellowship." What specific actions does this involve? Which segments of your fellowship need more encouragement to develop and utilize their gifts?

6. "Some churches don't grow simply because even if they have the money, they are too reluctant to spend it." In how many different ways could your congregation invest for growth? Which three stand out as the most important?

7. "If you want your church to grow, you have to invest more time." How much time do you already invest each month? How could you use that time more effectively? Who could help you maximize the impact of your time investments? How much more time could you invest for growth without compromising other biblical priorities?

11

. . . And Can We Afford It?

THE PRICE OF GROWTH—making changes, equipping workers, using gifted people, spending money, and investing more time. After counting these costs, are you still willing to pursue church growth for the glory of God? If your answer is yes, consider five more costs before you begin.

Loss of Intimacy

As a congregation begins to grow it loses intimacy. Many smaller fellowships don't want to grow because they naturally enjoy their intimate family atmosphere and don't want to lose it. Congregations of fifty, sixty, or seventy people might have an unconscious fear of growth, especially if they have maintained the same size for several years.

When a church begins to grow some people will say, "I used to know everyone. Now I don't. It makes me uncomfortable." Others will say, "Before we got so large I could spot visitors, but not anymore."

An assembly we helped establish in Alberta experienced this loss of intimacy, too. For the first three years the entire congregation of fifty people enjoyed an annual overnight retreat. Those were fantastic times! As we grew we couldn't find a location large enough for an all-church retreat, so we replaced our annual retreat with a six-hour annual meeting and meal. Yes, we lost some intimacy. But the alternative would have been loss of those newcomers we had come to love and appreciate.

It's natural for us to enjoy—even cherish—intimacy. But God can keep us from loving intimacy more than we love the world that is dying without Christ! Loss of intimacy is a small price to pay for church growth.

As we discussed in chapter six, small groups are effective tools which help retain intimacy in a growing church. Some of our mid-week growth groups enjoy more intimate fellowship than many small churches.

Loss of Influence

Another reason some people resist growth is the potential loss of personal influence in the congregation. As a church grows, some people will lose power. Their opinions won't be as influential, and their families won't be as prominent as they once were. This is uncomfortable, but inevitable.

Some people have difficulty coping with that loss of influence. Consciously or unconsciously, they resist growth. And although that resistance is never verbalized, visitors no longer sense that they are welcome.

If you are that key person, or you are part of that powerful family, recognize the responsibility you have before God. Until you let go of your influence, you could be blocking the church's growth.

Loss of Comfort

Other people resist growth because it makes them feel uncomfortable—another cost of church growth. Growth can be like buying new shoes. The old shoes feel comfortable, and the new ones don't. But the new shoes are better for you, and soon will feel good to your feet.

A long-time church attender with a large family once told me, "Last Sunday I was talking between meetings and forgot about the time. When I finally tried to sit with my family, the auditorium was so crowded that we couldn't sit together. I don't think I like church growth!"

Of course he said it in jest, but some people do react negatively to the small inconveniences resulting from growth. Someone else parks in your spot or sits in your pew. You feel uncomfortable with those new people who dress differently, talk differently, and act differently. Life is not as predictable now. Your group is not as comfortable as it once was.

But do we go to church to have our own way? Of course not! Christ called us to serve, and that is rarely comfortable.

Taking Risks

Church growth involves taking some risks. If we don't introduce any new activities, methods, or people, then we aren't taking any risks. Life without risks is comfortable and safe, but it's also stagnant.

I mentioned earlier that our fellowship in Florida took a risk by introducing a Christmas Eve service. We expected fifty to attend, but 120 came! If only fifteen had come, we might have considered it a failure. But we took a risk, and the results were tremendous.

I worked with one congregation for about a year, and we

saw tremendous growth. But in this small town church I took a risk by planning a retreat for married couples. They had never had such a retreat before, and none of the people responded. The retreat idea was a flop! However, in that same congregation I tried eight or ten other new ideas, and they were all successful. If you seek church growth, you will try new things. If some of them fail, they fail. So what! Don't let failure or potential failure discourage you from trying.

Some people believe that failure so dishonors God that they're afraid to try anything new. But I think God would say, "Don't be afraid to try. Don't be afraid to fail." A growing fellowship needs men and women who will say, "I'd rather attempt something great for God and fail, than attempt nothing and succeed."

Our growing church in Florida became too crowded during our Sunday morning service. We needed more room so we took the risk of starting a second Sunday morning service. We held our breaths. What if no one came to the new 8:30 a.m. service? But we had to take that risk. We rejoiced when 100 people attended our first early service. When we took that risk, God blessed us with continued growth.

A growing church isn't afraid to risk. Be willing to risk failure by asking young men and women or people new to the congregation to serve. Don't think, "That new fellow might fail; let's not ask him to serve in this area." Take a risk. Give him an opportunity to serve God and to try out his gifts. You may be surprised and encouraged by the results.

Solving Problems

When people come to Christ, they bring their problems with them. And when they join your fellowship, they bring those problems, too. Part of growth is helping people solve their problems.

At Palm Bible Chapel we are involved in evangelism. We find that the majority of newly converted adults have led difficult lives. Many are divorced, and some are already in their second or third marriages. As we reach these people for Christ, we encounter diverse family and marital problems.

We counsel people whose lives have been shattered by divorce—people who are thinking about dating again. They need biblical answers to questions that seem unanswerable. We counsel people who are struggling with alcohol and drug abuse. These people have been born again, but they are still enslaved by their old lives. How can we minister to people with such scars?

The easiest way to avoid dealing with such problems is to hang a neon sign on your church that reads: "Only long-time Christians welcome here." Unfortunately, many churches unconsciously convey this attitude, and non-Christians and new Christians are quick to sense it.

If you want to reach the people God loves, you must cope with problems and with problem people. The church is a hospital which serves the walking wounded—people who have been healed in Christ but still bear deep scars.

Proverbs 14:4 says, "Where there are no oxen, the manger is empty, but from the strength of an ox comes an abundant harvest." If you keep the oxen—the people with problems—out of the barn, your barn will be clean, but it will also be empty. But if you get involved in evangelism—if you begin to reach new people and bring them into the church—the barn will get messy. But what a worthwhile harvest you'll have!

Too often we focus on clean barns instead of an abundant harvest. We pray and give to further the harvest in foreign lands, where the barns are sometimes messy but where the churches grow. Here at home we are often content just to keep the barn clean. Even though we are surrounded by hurting people, we fail to reach out to them. We must follow Christ's example by reaching out to those who desperately need a shepherd.

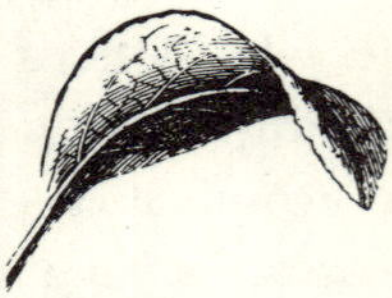

Study Questions

1. "As a congregation begins to grow it loses intimacy." Why do we enjoy and cherish intimacy? How might your congregation retain intimacy as it grows?

2. "As a church grows, some people will lose power." How influential are you and your family within your congregation? How much influence are you willing to relinquish so that your congregation can grow?

3. "Growth can be like buying new shoes." How can discomfort be minimized as your congregation grows?

4. "Leaders must be willing to risk failure." What risks has your congregation taken in the last years? Is your church better for having taken those risks? How? What new risks should your leadership consider taking within the next twelve months?

5. "Part of growth is helping people solve their problems." Where do people in your congregation turn for help? How could you better minister to those who hurt?

12

It's Worth the Price!

THERE'S A POPULAR SAYING in the business world: "Show me a man who takes no inventories, and I'll show you a man who goes bankrupt." It's not easy to evaluate yourself or your church. The more you are involved and the more you have invested, the more difficult it is to evaluate.

But unless we want to go bankrupt in terms of growth, we must get on our knees and evaluate ourselves thoroughly before God. How desperately we need God's help to see ourselves and our service for him as he sees it! As members of the body of Christ, we must pray, evaluate, and plan. Ask God to let his Spirit fill you with his love for the lost world around you and with the power to reach that world for Jesus Christ.

One day each of us will give an account to God for what he has done to help Christ's church grow. What have you accomplished? Are you committed to sharing the gospel? Are you committed to making disciples? Are you committed to church growth? Or are you a pew-sitter, just observing the activity around you as if you were viewing a play?

The cost of church growth *is* high. No wonder so many fellowships don't grow. Although people don't consciously say, "We refuse to pay the price of growth," many have made that decision. They refuse to change; they refuse to sacrifice. They refuse to pay the price. And the result? Stagnating churches!

Charles Swindoll compares church growth to remodeling your home: it always takes longer than you planned. It costs more than you figured. It is messier than you anticipated. And it requires greater determination than you ever expected.

J. Robertson McQuilken, president of Columbia Bible College, visted several growing churches in Japan with Donald McGavren, a pioneer of the church growth movement. McQuilken was puzzled that each of the growing churches cited a different reason for its growth. One cited commitment to prayer; another claimed it was excellent organization; and a third credited a movement of the Holy Spirit. So McQuilken asked McGavren what he believed was the secret to Japanese church growth.

"There's no mystery there," McGavren replied. "What do they all have in common? They all *expect to grow,* and they *go out and do it!"*

But why should we be so intently committed to conversion growth? Here are a few of the best reasons:

God Wants Church Growth

God loves the world! He sent his Son to die for mankind, and now he commands us to proclaim this good news to all people.

So when our churches fail to reach others for Christ, we are directly disobeying him. Because God wants our fellowships to grow, we should want it, too. In obedience to Christ, and motivated by his love, we should be involved in church growth.

The World Needs Church Growth

How desperately the world needs salvation! The majority of North Americans are heading for a Christless eternity. How can we ignore their urgent need? More than 175 million Americans do not know Christ as Savior yet. What are you doing to reach those in your own community?

The effectiveness of evangelism by the church in North America will directly affect our missionary outreach around the world. Only growing churches can send effectively equipped missionaries into the world. Overseas outreach is necessarily connected to the strength of churches here at home that send missionary workers. We are *commanded* to reach the world for Jesus Christ.

We Need Church Growth

We need to grow so that we can bring in the people around us. As the church grows, it develops the workers and resources needed to reach a lost and needy world. They are reason enough, but we also need church growth for ourselves.

Few things are more exciting than being involved in a church that grows and impacts its community for Jesus Christ. One of the greatest remedies for spiritual dullness is the tremendous personal benefit in growth—seeing people confess Christ, hearing their testimonies, becoming involved with them, and leading them to Christian maturity. *We all need growth.*

Eternal Rewards Are at Stake

Sometimes we pour all of our energy into church maintenance—activities that keep the local church functioning smoothly. These activities may be worthwhile, but they do nothing to extend Christ's kingdom.

Someone once referred to Christians as people who are busy rearranging the deck chairs on the Titanic! We make things tidier and more comfortable while the ship is sinking and lives are in grave danger.

The apostle Paul warned that each of us must appear before the judgment seat of Christ, that each one may receive what is due him (2 Cor. 5:10).

Paul also writes that what we do "will be revealed with fire, and the fire will test the quality of each man's work. If what he has built survives, he will receive his reward" (1 Cor. 3:13-14).

I urgently challenge you to invest wisely. Those who invest their energy, time, money, and gifts in New Testament church growth will certainly be rewarded. More people must be our goal. Growth *is* worth the price!

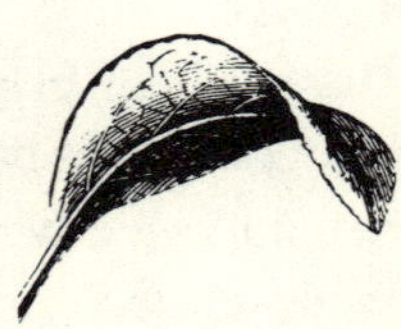

Study Questions

1. "Although people don't consciously say, 'We refuse to pay the price of growth,' many have made that decision." Why do some say "no" to numerical growth? Does your congregation want to grow? Why or why not?

2. "Those who invest their energy, time, money, and gifts in in New Testament church growth will certainly be rewarded." What investment are you making to extend Christ's kingdom? What reward do you expect?

For further information on church growth, write to:

Interest Ministries
218 West Willow Avenue
Wheaton, Illinois 60187